Diaries of a Poet

by

Heidi L. Hart

RoseDog Books
PITTSBURGH, PENNSYLVANIA 15238

RoseDog Books
585 Alpha Drive, Suite 103
Pittsburgh, PA 15238
Visit our website at www.rosedogbookstore.com

ISBN: 979-8-89211-387-8
eISBN: 979-8-89211-884-2

Poem Guide

HEIDI L. HART

Here Kitty Kitty

Today was really hard for me
To try and use restraint
You wrapped your arms around me
And I started feeling faint

At that point I was safe
From any problem on its way
Just having you there to hold
Starts and ends a beautiful day

Sometimes we touch on subjects
That are better not discussed
So I'll quickly change the topic
So your feelings don't get crushed

We've got something good
I could not bare to let go
I just have so many feelings
Its so much to let them show

When I wake up in the morning
To that smile on your face
It makes it so much easier
To get up and start my day

I get so far down
Every step you walk away
Just like a pent up tiger
All I want is just to play

Here kitty, kitty
Makes me weak in the knees
So I crawl across the floor
Intensely begging, God please

For this one wish of happiness
I'd give most anything
You bring me such joy in life
You make the birdies sing

I just keep walking everyday
With the love you give to me
Any problems that cause blindness
You knock em down and make me see

You are the power
That carries me through
Lights up my life
And shows me the truth

Feeling U

I dance among the waterfalls
And swim straight through the streams
It doesn't matter where I go
I see you in my dreams

I'm weak when I'm alone
I need you here with me
You give me clear vision
Without you, I can not see

I can't think a single thought
You're always there, I see your face
When I feel the burn of love
Up in my eyes like mace

I don't ever want to let you go
You bring life where there was not
You take my slowed down life
And bring it quickly to a trot

One quick look into your eyes
Puts me safely in a trance
No one should have the power
That you put into a glance

You drive me crazy in an instant
And make me shake in just one more
You've taken a lost little girl
Picked her up, and showed her the door

What you truly mean to me
I could not express to you
You could never understand
Just what it is you do

You put me on a cloud
And lay me back with ease
Don't ever walk away my love
You've got me down here on my knees

I live to love you
It just feels right
If only I could hold you
When I go to sleep at night

Do you understand, what you've done
By giving this to me
We build it up, like nothing else
And it's stronger than the sea

HEIDI L. HART

Interpretation

What does it all mean
Will we ever know
Does emotion travel parallel
With persecution in tow

Go ahead and ask yourself
But don't expect today
You'll get the answers of tomorrow
Sneaked to you in any way

I love, but do I not...
Care in that such way
Does demeanor separate value
Split your life of from your day

Weakness breeds confusion
Blinds those who have never seen
If one can not muster will
Life and love shall split between

An apology of inner being
To preserve time in solemn right
Upon one's decent from high
Your heart and head will always fight

Belief is like the frame
In which questions can not shake
Stand in formal attitude
What does decision really make

So is the way of what was
And strong is the way of now
Never step to destiny
And expect to reveal how

Dance with purity on your shoulder
Letting conviction be your guide
Confine your serious thought
Completion proves you really tried

Live, to find sweet peace
Love, to have it all
Never discourage final worth
For dreams shatter when they fall

Take it for the truth
Better words not to be found
Drive for one's perfection
While valiant triumphs come around

HEIDI L. HART

Melt

To die from desire
Is to live by your heart
Seeking inner passion
Moving forth but not to part

Melt within the motion
Let your body flow
Indulgence is so fine
To love true, is to know

I can not concern myself
With what politicians think
A body buzz that doesn't quit
Lusting life like it's a drink

You burn me with a single touch
Leave me begging for one more
I puddlize in front of you
And then spread across the floor

How can one ever imagine
Such a feeling can't exist!
You could study it forever
And never really get the gist

With power of suggestion
You turn me inside out
You make my body scream
And it drives my soul to shout

I start to tingle when you speak
Your words empower sweet relief
No one on the outside sees
Because they have their own belief

The power that you give me
Makes me thirst for nothing more
It pains me when you walk away
And exit through that door

My heart is like a window
My feelings fragile glass
And you my little kitten
Looking straight into my past

This last prayer to hold you near
Keep you safe inside my shell
We shall dance like this forever
Together as one we start to melt

HEIDI L. HART

I Only Hope

I'm getting called a cheater
For a crime that's uncalled for
I use to have it solid
Now she wants to walk out the door

There's nothing I want more
Then to just erase myself
Cremate my worn out body
And put me on a shelf

I never seem to get it right
No matter what I do
I guess I screwed up this time
I did not mean to hurt you

Sometimes I feel cursed
With these things I go through
I think we could get past this
But I don't know, if you want to

I'm not sure if you still want me
So I take it blow by blow
And if it comes down to it
And you want, then I will go

I have only happy memories
In which I can't let go
I would like to make some more
Just wanted to let you know

I can't see how you love me
And want me gone at the same time
I could use a drink right now
A Tequila with salt and lime

I want things back to the way they were
I need you in my life
Nothings really changed my dear
I still want you to be my wife

A friend with real strong feelings
Is what has put me here
I didn't see it coming
I want to be with you my dear

I only hope its not too late
To keep you by my side
Because without you in my life
I might as well have died

HEIDI L. HART

You Make Me

I love that show The L Word
It's the best show I have seen
But some of the shit that goes on
By some of the girls in that show, are mean

Today I had to eat it
I'm told I'm no better than them
It hurt me to hear those words
Magnified to the power of 10

I can't help this inner thought
That I might lose you still
My perfect world is falling apart
And I'm starting to lose my will

I don't wanna see it
Any other way
I wanna wake up in the morning
And have you there throughout the day

I feel like such an asshole
Yet I haven't done a thing
I love you so damn much
I wish I could afford your ring

This love is like a marriage
And forever is my goal
I don't want to give this up
I want to give you my soul

There is not much left of me
But all of me is yours
The only regret I have
Is that I couldn't give you more

I like this thing we have
You and I, we seem to fit
Your everything I'm not
I'm the ball and you're the mitt

I like to sleep with you at night
And then wake up in the morn
See that smile on your face
Then curl up in our spoon form

You make me smile when I can't
Think happy thoughts when I'm down
You've taught me oh, so much
Learn to smile and not frown

HEIDI L. HART

It's Real

How is it I could know
If there's a chance I am mistaken
I think every step you take back
It leaves my heart just breaking

I've had a lot to drink today
And yet, you're still on my mind
I don't think I can clear it out
In a way I guess that's fine

I get so damn confused
But it does come back to me
Every time I think its gone
My heart, it makes me see...

I can't run away from this
It's me, on an average day
It leaves me feeling drunk
The twisted words, it makes me say

Do I really want to hurt like this
I think I really do
If it means me having happiness
Forever, I'm with you

It makes me feel so free...
To love so hard and true
With my back against the wall
I'm still right here in front of you

No one can kill these feelings
That I have built up deep inside
Alone I stand in darkness
Fot the tears that I have cried

You stand there proclaiming love
That you hold deep in fear
That you might lose one day
I haven't walked away my dear

I hold you so close to my heart
For there is no other place for you
Cuz deep inside, my love
I know the feeling I have is true

So be strong and true to you
Cuz on that you can depend
You can't lose me forever
Because I'm here until the end

HEIDI L. HART

Can't Drown It

I'm driving through the desert
I'm on the way to hell
I saw that look upon your face
Jumped the bridge, misjudged and fell

I've tried with out success
To make this all be good
But apparently I'm wrong
Not having done just what I should

I get a little tipsy
When I think of what could be
If only I could steer the car
To thee instructions left for me

I never get it right
Pain, is all I have mastered
Leaving hatred in the wing
As I get called a bastard

Maybe its true enough
And I'm living in denial
Whatever it is this time
I feel as though our loves on trial

Back to the original thought
Of never getting it right
It must be true enough
Cuz I sleep alone at night

Right now I just don't know
Where I'm gonna go from here
I should stop off at the pub
Drown my thoughts with a little beer

I can't drown this out
I've been trying to all day
It pops right back up
Without the words to say

Like I could find all the answers
In this bottle at this time
If you lower me a straw
Maybe I could start to climb

Whatever bridge I cross
Consequence is waiting there
Misery dances on my shoulders
Because it moves without a care

Noodle

I got asked the question
Just what it is I do
"To make these people fall
So deeply in love with you?"

I said that I don't know
I can't even see that straight
I talked to my ex of 8 years today
He said forever he would wait

I feel like a demon
With the power of true love
I don't like this feeling
I wish I could rise above

I cause everybody pain
To reach me in this way
It's everything I can do
Just to make it through my day

I think God is testing me
To see if I will fall apart
Here's my warning to the world
Put a fence around your heart

It should never be this way
I want a semi normal life
A house out on a farm
My one son, and just one wife

Do you think it's cause I am
To fricken nice to hate
Maybe we could sit and talk
And prevent the words, too late

I just want this feeling gone
It's killing me in ways
I haven't had peace of mind
In, I've lost count of the days

I am just one person
On the track to loneliness
Just wishing you were here with me
I am in need of your caress

My heart is pounding now
In slow motion I shall die
There's no way out of this hell
No matter what I try

HEIDI L. HART

Confusions Path

The drink that starved my freedom
Stole my life and love alike
It walks in blind man's shoes
And moves as fast as a race bike

Dodging trees, and jumping stumps
You think you have it all
If you don't catch that jump just right
I guarantee you'll fall

You can't play with fire crackers
And not know you'll get burned
Things can get so ugly
When the table's getting turned

Stupid is the way
So treacherous consequence
When I made that left hand turn
And stepped outside the fence

I hope you'll be there for me
Because I won't hold back the tears
It's hard to lose the game
And overcome your fears

Everybody needs a friend
When their trapped in a low
This time is the worst
I feel my heart could explode

Times not on my side
I don't think it's ever been
It makes me fear for Franklin
Cause the boy is only 10

He's been stuck with my mistakes
No matter what they are
I hope as he gets older
They don't cause a mental scar

At this point I just don't know
How to put it all in line
I need to figure it out
Because I'm running out of time

I'll just keep looking forward
Because that's how it works
Life's not provided me a map
So I'll have to straighten out the quirks

HEIDI L. HART

No Such Thing

I had somebody tell me
That they don't believe in love
Like anyone's that free to think
That they could rise above

You can't fight the feeling
When it grabs you by the hand
An emotion un-sequestered
While you try to make your stand

Not willing to repent
When there's a chance of being strong
I just can't turn away
I've had this feeling way to long

We set ourselves up
To take another hit
When you get your feelings hurt
It makes you just wanna spit

Just cause you don't like the pain
That love tends to put us through
Doesn't mean you can deny
That love is really true

As I walk this road of life
And love catches up with me
I can't see how you care
I feel like a demon seed

Sometimes you live inside yourself
So you can avoid the paid
I don't think I blame you
No one wants to feel insane

But to claim that its not real
What a flippin thing to say
I know that I can prove you wrong
But it takes more than a day

You give up inside to quickly
What are you running from
You turn to darkness for the answer
Why don't you step into the sun

Perfections like the Tango
It takes two, to make it go
You get out what you put in
Make an effort, to let it show

A Piece

In the back of my mind
I have so much to say
But to put it, into words
I just can't find a way

I'm afraid to say out loud
That I can't handle stress
Every time I start it
My whole life becomes a mess

A chicken I might be
And for this I will burn
One can not die from this
But make you wish it was your turn

A turn for what you ask
Just a chance to understand
You make your own decisions
Does God really have a plan

I suffer on my own
I am why, I'm here
Born with to much love
This is a curse of fear

It's the same for others
That live a life like mine
A heart that's way to soft
So it gets crushed up fine

Standing in the courtroom
I guess guilty is my plea
I shall serve my time in prison
Crime of loving openly

I give everyone a piece of me
But sometimes it's not enough
So I sit here in punishment
Because I didn't want it rough

Why must all this be
There's got to be another way
A set of words I haven't said
At the right time, on the right day

Looking back is scary
And I feel I can't move forth
With all these feelings rushing up
Coming from an unknown source

HEIDI L. HART

Unsaid Words

There's something I need to tell you
And it's eating me up inside
The longer I hold it in
The more tears I will have cried

I don't want to feel like this
And I don't think I need to
If I could get this off my chest
And say what I need to say to you

Then I wouldn't have this feeling
Of not using my one chance
My body language maker is broke
I can't say what I need in just a glance

This fear I hold right now
Of being scared and all alone
Not knowing if you'd talk to me
If I called you on the phone

I miss the closeness that we had
And knowing I can't have it back
It causes me these unsaid words
By the minute do they stack

Even if I had the chance
To say just what I need
The fear of your rejection
On my mind this thing shall feed

I really shouldn't feel this way
But it is who I've become
The one that cares to much
I think my work at trying's done

I wish I could set it down
And let that set me free
But enclosed I shall remain
In my head its only me

I've been sworn to this
Unto me by our dear lord
Life and love were labeled right
When called a double edge sword

So unsaid words are what I'm left with
It just seems the only way
It kills me to lose it all
I hold memories of a better day

HEIDI L. HART

That's All I've Left

Time, it stands so still
When you try to move forth
Always someone there to shake the map
When your planning out your course

How are you supposed to make it
With the problems in the air
So thick that you can't see
In 2 directions, you shall tear

You want to take the easy route
It seems the only way to go
But it leads to pain as well
Just incase you didn't know

I wish, I wish, I wish…
Frustrations setting in
It doesn't matter what I do
I know that I can't win

I think I knew from the beginning
That I was in a losing game
I still chose to play
So now I shall face the shame

Shame of a lost friendship
But there's nothing I can do
I hold onto these memories
Cuz that's all I've left of you

Am I to blame for what has happened
I can't help but feel it is
Long term cut to nothing
In one quick simple wiz

I hold regret upon my shoulders
Yet, I guess I must get past...
The feeling of a cure
Cuz this thing we had, has crashed

I'm gonna learn to stand again
And not live my life in fear
That's not so easy for me sometimes
But this time I'll have to dear

I'm not looking for any trouble
It seems to find me on its own
The chance of hiding from it
One more time I've seem to blown

HEIDI L. HART

Why U So Angry

I have this crazy talent
I make people mad with ease
I don't really mean to man
Lighten up a little please

Our lives are way to busy
For perfections point of view
I'm anything but perfect
Does that not seem right to you

Every time I turn around
I'm waiting for a fight
We might not have this problem
If you weren't always right

It sucks to live like this
When its so easy to smile
There's no sense in acting like this
It just makes you seem so vial

Maybe we could start all over
I'll introduce myself again
I don't think that you noticed
That I call you my friend

I will quickly turn around
So that you can recompose
Calm yourself down a bit
And lower that raised nose

I'm not mad at you
What was it that I did
I have not been treated like this
Since I was just a kid

I wish I had a mirror
So that you could see yourself
You need to tone it down
Put that shit up on the shelf

That natural blush your wearing
Is such a pretty red
But I can't help but think
That inside you wish me dead

It's gonna be alright
No matter what you say
Cuz when you wake up tomorrow
It will be a brand new day

HEIDI L. HART

Life's Jungle

Ask if your not sure
Uncertainty leads to circumstance
Unless you like that drama
Then you can dance that silly dance

For me its not the same
I'm not kosher with it all
I've been set up to many times
And I'm tired of taking the fall

I walk right into the trap
Like a mouse in search of cheese
I can't and will not try again
No matter how you beg and plead

I just can't grasp the notion
That you want me around
I feel like I'm the problem
No bigger challenge to be found

Open up that door to life
Take one step forward and hold on
You'll get your chance to ride
That shooting star you sat upon

Never knowing what you'll find
As curiosity draws you in
You start this game illiterate
To when it is you'll reach the end

The rules are bound to change a bit
But some will stay the same
You'll run into some problems
And you'll have to take the blame

It won't stop you from trying
If it does the game is over
Luck has nothing to do with it
There's no such thing as magic clover

I don't say this to cause fear
It's just the way it is
The jungle that we walk through
To receive out fatal kiss

Laugh and smile for me
Even if it seems to hard
I will be here with you
Clear through the harder part

HEIDI L. HART

A Half Life

What was God thinking
When he presented me
I can't help but find mistakes
Imagination just ran free

I'm not sure where to start
On the things that I've found wrong
I'm currently trapped inside myself
It makes forever seem so long

It's painful in the mornings
When I wake to see this face
Only 26 short years in
My smiles gone without a trace

I guess it's not the half of it
My decisions are the worst
They all backfire in my face
It's like, I was born cursed

I've been living by a theory
That I'm not real sure is right
I have to many bolts loose
That I, just cant get tight

Everything I build just breaks
So why do I give it so much time
I'm breaking down to far
Making my transition into slime

I've been hurt to many times
To even look ahead today
My self esteem is gone
And I'm losing my strength to pray

Is it time for last requests
I'd like steak, with a dinner roll
Then we can drive out to the cemetery
And you can dig my hole

I don't want to take this route
But yet I'm lost without a prayer
Surrounded by the worst of things
And not a one could give a care

I place myself down at your feet
I am at your mercy now
In hopes that you have time
To show a sista how

HEIDI L. HART

My Muse

Once again you're here
I am weak and you are strong
We travel down this road
You are right and I am wrong

I have so much left to learn
About this thing that I've become
I will give it my best effort
To find myself, and then be done

Maybe I could change
This course that I been through
And at the end I shall smile
While I'm holding on to you

My muse of inner thought
As you shine upon me light
You make it all make sense
On the inside it feels right

But alone I hold this feeling
That you will go away
It will be the death of me
If I'm forced to face that day

Lost among the tumbleweed
We set forth one more time
Not to lose my concentration
Cuz you are my muse of rhyme

You make my thoughts flow clearly
Just like they were always there
Sometimes they cause pain
But that is my cross to bare

Alone when facing issues
It attacks the inner me
Together we will stand
It is then that I will see

Everything I want in life
Is just a phallic dream
Because without you by my side
I'm just a bulb without a beam

For all I wish the best
And I hope your dreams come true
For me its not the same
I'm in the dark waiting for you

HEIDI L. HART

Running Down

Every minute that passes by
Is one more we can't get back
As I lay down on the pillow
Those minutes really start to stack

You turn around for just a minute
And your world has rearranged
Things have happen to you
That you wish that you could change

Followed closely by this figure
But you can not see a face
Up and gone into the shadows
In the darkness is his place

You now approach things differently
Hoping you can find the path
Without a light to guide you
You are bound to feel his wrath

The feeling's growing stronger
But you know you must move forth
Praying god will send the answer
So you can get back on your course

Ticking as the clock does
In its ever changing ways
Time speeds up when things are good
And slows down on judgement day

You can't help but get discouraged
When walls pop up around
Like a rat trapped in a maze
No way out, is to be found

I wasted to much time
And I'm still lost without a clue
Or am I only lost
Because I'm not there with you

You've got to help me out
Before this comes to a stop
I know I can be taught
To deal, and come out on top

Sleep with one eye open
Don't let a minute pass you by
Cuz you can't fix your problems
If you don't give it an honest try

HEIDI L. HART

My Wish To God

Sit and look my dear
Deep into my eyes
For the love I hold for you
In no way could I disguise

Go together with me
And forever we shall stay
Lost in this love we've built
Living happily day after day

When you look at me
I can see a love so deep
As it pours through my skin
And to my heart it slowly seeps

When you start to smile
I begin to understand
This love we have between us
Is vibrant and so grand

When you reach out and touch me
My body starts to melt
Feelings this strong and true
Are almost sinful to be felt

I couldn't ask for more
As I stand and look at you
I know that God has blessed me
With a love that is so true

How did I end up here
Lost and tripping on myself
High on life like I've been hit
By a can of greatness, off the shelf

I wanna take you by the hand
And lay you softly down to sleep
Whisper, sweet nothings in your ear
Until your off and counting sheep

When you wake up in the morning
Best believe you'll find me there
Laying right beside you love
Rubbing you softly with such care

This is my wish to God
Please just let me live this life
This one happy journey
As I take her as my wife

HEIDI L. HART

A Poet's Level

All or nothing
Is that's what I get
Then on that decision
I shall sit

You can't rush perfection
When you call it a friend
Cuz I'm telling you now
It will come to an end

What I have with you
I could never replace
With any amount of time
Or any amount of space

Why risk forever
By pushing for one more
Can't you see, my love
I'm up against the door

I don't want to walk away
From what it is we share
No one else can say a word
And get me to give a care

We are on a level
No one else can understand
They are in the valley
As we crawl to higher land

I don't want to think
About the end of you and I
To give up just like that
Without giving it a try

Right now is where we are
And the future's where we'll be
To say that I know how
Is just not something I can see

When we sit and talk
I feel somewhat at ease
That some one understands
Why I'm down here on my knees

Crying one more tear
For one last painful burn
That I've had thrown at me
It's relief that I shall yearn

HEIDI L. HART

Truth's Silent Words

One very special moment
For one very special girl
Cuz I cant put into words
How it is you are my world

I live to see you smile
It keeps my life on track
I can't go on without you
You are my life, and that's a fact

When I find myself alone
I know your never far away
You fill my head with happy thoughts
And that's what gets me through my day

I fall every time I see you
Right back in to your arms
It is there that I feel safe
From any and all of life's harms

You pick me up when I am down
Push me forward when in fear
You help me find the answer
No matter what I need my dear

It is hard for me to sit
And bring silent words to light
Being the deepest of emotions
Inside and out they just feel right

Happiness and love
Seems to always get us there
To that place where all is good
To love free without a care

Place your hand in mine
Let's, let love lead the way
On the journey to forever
Locked in the moment of that day

Smile one more time for me
It makes my heart just melt
I can't say there's stronger feelings
In my life that I have felt

So for you truths silent words
And in them you can trust
For had I never said them
They would've built until I bust

HEIDI L. HART

Keep It Steady

I guess I've done it
One more time
I have committed
A silent crime

I hate it when that happens
Cause your never really sure
What it is you've done
So how can you find a cure

I can't give it to much thought
Because it will eat me alive
I can't take that kind of pressure
Cuz I'm just out to survive

At some point I'll work it out
And I know I'll come around
I will give you time to chill
So a solution can be found

If they really care about you
They would not treat you this way
For any given reason
On any given day

Take a breath my friends
I'll be here when you are ready
In your mind you break it up
But in mine, I keep it steady

If you really need to vent
Or, just sit back a minute
Go right ahead my dear
I'll be here when you are finished

You can't expect to have it all
It's grand when you get some
Patience helps us out
To reach our goals before we're done

Look at it from one more angle
Maybe it will bring to light
The things you need to know
To get you through the night

If you get down
Give me a call
I'll be here to catch you
When you take a fall

HEIDI L. HART

Forbidden Love

I have all these feelings
But I'm not suppose to care
I have all this, immense love
But I'm not suppose to share

When I find myself alone
Its you that's on my mind
But when I go looking for you
Its not you that I find

I yearn for something more
But I never get my way
My search still pushes on
In hopes, I will get my day

When I'm near you my sweet love
I can't picture anything else
But when you walk away my dear
I'm to put my heart, on the shelf

It doesn't work like that for me
Because I love you all the time
I don't think your being fair
When did love become a crime

I would give most anything
Just to have you by my side
Yet, I'm still left here waiting
With all these tears I've cried

I feel that if you loved me
As much as I loved you
You would let me love you freely
And show you, this love is true

Just give me one short minute
I will wipe out all your fears
For once you see the truth in it
I will cry no more sadness tears

My love is unconditional
I know yours would be the same
Love happens on its own
But yet, I'm still absorbing blame

Let me walk you from the sadness
And show you the light of love
I don't like the word forbidden
Cuz I think we can rise above

HEIDI L. HART

Blind Justice

I'm sitting here shaking
As I start to write
I know I'm headed
For my biggest fight

It's not with a who
Please don't ask me why
The battles with me
Myself and I

My reason is strong
My intention so true
I can't trust my secret
Not even to you

I must be alone
When this shit hits the fan
The grounds are unsafe
You could call it quick sand

It made so much sense
When I started out
But it's shaded somehow
And that's caused me some doubt

I would ask the question
If you wanted me to
But you know the answer
Would stupefy you

Time and again
It's the same fucking game
Someone pointing fingers
Leads to someone taking blame

We're not going there
Not in that way
The blame is on me
This is my judgement day

I'm going to hell
But its not a surprise
At least not to me
I've seen through these eyes

I've stepped over the line
For the very last time
I'm getting my punishment
For committing the crime

First Contact

I received a text last night
Then back and forth they went
You could feel the hatred growing
With every message sent

If you were to take your average man
He would tell you this was great
To have two women fighting over him
Like it was some debate

Not me, I don't find joy in this
Watching them tear each other to shreds
Waiting on the outcome of this
Is what all 3 of us really dreads

I'm sure for different reasons
We all want different things
Happiness revolves us all but me
I guess we'll see what this fight brings

It's the same for me day in day out
No inner peace is to be found
I still feel like I will be alone
When resolution comes around

The one I've always been with
Swears she gonna lose her mind
I wish that I could help
I love her, but I am blind

They both assume the form of death
But not quite in the same way
It doesn't really matter though
Both presence revealed, on my final day

Anyone who wants my life
Please step up to the bat
I will give you quick report
On just where your life is at

Maybe you can make some sense
Of this mess that I have made
I've really trapped a tiger here
Are you sure you wanna trade

It has paused for just a moment
I will have to get back to you
When I have a better theory
On what it is I need to do

HEIDI L. HART

The Price Of Insecurity

Try not to cry sweet love
As I become insane
I can't help but act this way
When I feel so much damn pain

A ping pong ball puts me pretty close
To what it is I feel I am
I'm gonna blow my head off
Just because I know I can

Fuck it all, its just not real
You can't make me believe
That happiness is reachable
That's an idea I can't conceive

I'm letting go of everything
I can't hold on to it no more
I'll take very little with me
When I walk out that door

I do want you to understand
No regrets will go with me
I loved you so damn much
I guess you just didn't see

I'm not real sure where I'm going
I will find out when I get there
It didn't have to be this way
I didn't really find it fair

Everything I built for us
Torn up before my eyes
I told you I could fix it
But you think I'm telling lies

I am running out of patience
And time, to find a cure
What is the point of fighting
If you believe your love is pure

Nothing else should matter now
We've pushed each other to the brink
Backed into a corner now
We'll wash our feelings down the sink

When you lay down to go to sleep
Don't let me cross your mind
It's not me that you need
Sanity's what you need to find

HEIDI L. HART

Inexcusable

Where to go from here
Is the question on my mind
I'm froze in this position
So no answer can I find

I let my mind wander free
And it cost me everything
My babydoll don't trust me now
I took the shine out of that ring

I am a thief of happiness
Yet I don't possess a drop
I should have walked away from it
But I just didn't stop

So for now I sit posted
Wondering if she will come back
Is her love for me still there
Can we get past, this crack

She doesn't have a good reason
But yet I wanna make it go
Every morning sleeping with fear
That she'll come home and tell me no

One day at a time
Is how its got to be
Because I screwed it up
I'll just have to wait and see

I am not usually quiet
But I have nothing to say
I know I made a mistake
Now I'll take it day by day

I can only hope time heals
All the pain that I have brought
Honesty was not good to me
Now it is repair that is sought

I'm sorry, just don't cover it
For the way I broke your heart
I drove you to insanity
And made you wanna part

So I will sit here until
You ask me to walk away
I can only hope I never
Have to face that day

HEIDI L. HART

The What If Game

The world is run
On a what if game
No matter how you look at it
The answers still the same

We can't control much at all
If we could that would be great
We'd never feel emotional pain
Or the jagged edge of fate

I am not as strong
As I would like to be
But I am slowly learning
How it is to see

Your not giving it much time
To get to where your gonna find
Everything you want in life
And people are never kind

So where's the silver lining
I think that's truly just a phrase
To confuse the simple people
And get through the longer days

There is no good to be had
From the bad that comes our way
Believing is what gets us there
And love is why we stay

What if, is just a thought
That causes butterfly effect
Its best not to toy
When its trouble you attract

I'm not sure what I'd change
For what the outcome might be
I don't like unknown answers
When your hanging by a string

Please give me one more chance
That's what it boils down to
When you can't have what you want
But it's still what you wanna do

Lets all what if
One more time
Mend the ladder
And start to climb

HEIDI L. HART

Dear Jane

I want so bad to hit rewind
So that I can slap myself
Before I do something wrong
To prevent the hardship felt

I never wanted anything
With anyone but you
I know the love we have
Is solid and so true

Nobody seems to understand
What it is we have together
We put our love upon the wind
And it floats, just like a feather

I have had these feelings for you
About 4 years and they are strong
Let me help you past this all
Problems never go on long

50-50 is the way to be
That is how we have to live
I am the bricks, you are the mortar
The makes our wall stand stiff

You can not let this change us
If it does, then they win
Giving up on such a love...
Of such a long time we've been in

I will be here when its through
To take your hand in mine
If it cost me everything we have
Right down to my last dime

Road blocks are bound to happen
You can't control that part
Just try to understand my love
These feelings I hold for you in my heart

If you have to walk away
I'll be here when you get back
If you decide you do not want me
Then I will start to pack

Whatever you decide my love
I am only here for you
I don't want to give you up
But I have to if you do

"28"

One more birthday
Come and gone
Started out so well
Ended like a country song

That's just the luck I have
Some how I guess I knew
By the end of the day
That I'd be down and blue

I attract way to much drama
I wanted it to go smooth
I should have planned it better
I don't know what I was trying to prove

28 is not quite 30
But bad is how it went
These moments of our younger years
Has got me totally spent

I'm trapped inside this body
With no release of mind
I only wanted happiness
And it's what I didn't find

I gave up and changed my number
So the burn would start to end
It never should have been this way
When these people call you friend

This shit is hardly over love
My birthdays just the start
You can't change feelings like a number
And expect their gonna part

For now I'm in a calm
And I'm in it all alone
I can't talk to anybody
At least, not through the phone

Fuck, I wanna scream
But it echo's back at me
It all feels like a mistake
That no one else can see

Screw it, today I'm 28
Tomorrow will be the same
If luck jumps to my side
I'll wake up without this pain

HEIDI L. HART

Opinion By Right

A needle in a haystack
By definition hard to find
With me it's a little different
Riding on a finer line

How can one, just confess
To being life's sharp spot
You think it's safely on the bottom
But its hiding at the top

A tiny hole caused from a pin
Only draws one drop of blood
But then it becomes infected
Leaving you face down in the mud

I hold this opinion of myself
As my life builds up strain
This phallic world we live in
I seem to be the source of pain

I hope to get past this view
To become what I know I can
It all gets a little worse
Before you can learn to stand

But still I just keep walking
On this journey to the end
Hoping somewhere along the way
I make and keep, at least one friend

It all seems so easy
To reach such a simple goal
Not with matters of the heart
That lead straight back to your soul

I know I take more blame
Than should ever be on me
It's easier that way
Then to make blind people see

I don't claim to have the answers
To the questions in the air
But I have to find them anyway
Just to prove I'll always care

I've gained the right to this opinion
It's how people make me feel
There to make me realize
That my situations real

HEIDI L. HART

The Hunters And The Hunted

What a rush I feel inside
I am sitting in a field
Like a deer come open season
With nothing there to shield

From one side then the other
I just know I'm gonna die
Running fast as I can go
I can't give up, and just not try

I got a blast of, "you're a bitch"
Followed by you can't make a decision
When you get hateful words like that
It makes you not wanna go on living

Do I think I'll find some clearing?
Where I might catch my breath
Not right now cause I'm still running
To prove, you can outrun death

I know I can't outrun my problems
That I'm not living in a dream
I'm just praying for some guiding light
Even if its, just a little gleam

At this point I'm just not sure
Of where all of this will go
I try not to look that far
I'm not sure yet I want to know

I stop and hide a moment
In this forest dark as night
Hoping I can slip past trouble
Long enough to make it right

I know what I have to do
And the road is very long
I'm going to stand and make it work
Cuz to not, would just be wrong

The blasts are slowing now
From one side they are done
I have to overcome some challenges
That would not be considered fun

But I am here me sweet
Just keep the headlights down
I do not need extra confusion
As we put this in the ground

HEIDI L. HART

Human Shield

What's up my little friend
You look a little lost
Can I help you out at all
To save some of the final cost

I can't stand to see you
Fighting with this everyday
No one should have to suffer
There's got to be another way

I will be your human shield
Take me with you when you go
So you'll never have to wonder
Be positive in the fact you know

I can't give out respect
That's still got to be earned
Always owed more then you get
We all get a little burned

Peace on earth is just a dream
That not everyone will reach
There's to many haters in this world
To many people wanna preach

When you drift off to sleep
Set me down on your nightstand
In case you need me through the night
I'll put up a fight so grand

When you wake up in the morning
Take a second look at you
Realize you are not alone
I'm doing all that I can do

Everyday you will grow stronger
And I will wean you from my help
Until you have it under control
And your doing it by yourself

You never really needed me
I'm only what made you feel good
But now that you have got it
I'll go back to where I should

Hold me somewhere deep inside
Bring me out when you are weak
So you can stay on the path
And find what it is you seek

HEIDI L. HART

Heartbreaker

You call me a heartbreaker
Maybe that is what I am
It was not my intention
Nor was it my plan

What ever I was thinking
A plan I just can't see
"Live everyday as though your last"
Famous words that spoke to me

I wake up each after noon
Hoping there will be no more
Hearts that I'll be breaking
Just by walking out my door

I can not help these people
When they start to fall in love
And I can not pick them up
They're on their own to rise above

I have to walk away from it
To let them do it on their own
They will find the road they need
I don't think they can be shown

It's not going to be easy
I never said it would
I just know it has to be like this
It's the only way it could

I was told once by a nurse
That I needed to be cloned
Can you see the issues with that
How many lives would end up blown

You can not clone a heartbreaker
And expect good things to come
I only mess things up you know
Having more than one is dumb

I want to say I'm sorry
But do I deserve the blame
I guess I really do
Or I would not feel this shame

I just don't have it in me
To be mean to protect you
I don't think I can do it
Even if you asked me to

HEIDI L. HART

Painful Words

You looked at me and said
"No more shall I'll write"
The pressures gonna build
In your head your gonna fight

Back when I was 16
I wrote for some relief
To let out some of the stress
It was never to deceive

You not writing is your will
I don't know what it does for you
Maybe you don't need relief
But me, I know I do

I could never put it down
It has become my crutch
To help me find the answers
It's bailed me out so much

No one really understands
The power of my pen
When I can't talk to anyone
These blank pages are my friend

Did you say it to cause pain
Knowing words are my outlet
Did you think I would bow down
Like I was just your pet

We pick up and move on
Cause there is no other way
What I use to call a friendship
Has just become another page

I know I will survive
I've been down this road before
I've lost a lot of friends
Because I could not give them more

Smile if that's what you need
Cuss my name when your alone
I can't believe it went this far
Cause you can't call me on the phone

Better if you call it that
But life don't come pain free
I won't always be your pain
But I guess for now it's me

HEIDI L. HART

Drawing A Blank

The words seem to have gone
The ones I like to use
They describe my life so well
So do these words I choose

I draw blanks round every corner
Come up short when day has past
Living in a house of kryptonite
I hope this does not last

Where has my inspiration gone
I feel like I'm trapped in a cage
To have my powers stripped away
Just causes me this intense rage

I now cry tears of powder
And love with a broken heart
I write with dried up pens
So I never get past start

Alone in this aggravation
Praying for a speck of light
I just want it to come back
Even if its not tonight

How could it just go away
Was it ever really there
Why do we get teased with talent
I'm not sure I find it fair

Did I abuse it in some way
Not say the words I needed to
Did I spend to much time lost
Amongst these pages without truth

Or maybe I spoke words of reason
Teaching deaf ears how to hear
And this is just a moment of silence
I am welling up a tear

I'm sure that its still there
Hiding just behind the wings
No way of knowing yet
We must see what the future brings

So here is where I'll sit
With my pen in hand
Waiting for that moment
I shall seize and make a stand

HEIDI L. HART

Pain Finds Reason

I sit here with blank emotion
I am not sure what to say
Was this something I needed to know
Then to find out in this way

I am so happy for you
Or is it that I'm sad
This might be all good
But then it might be bad

I have so many questions
But no desire to ask
I don't really want to hear
You slide on another mask

I don't know who I am
O.M.G. I'm so damn lost
Your right I couldn't see
So I will eat the final cost

You gave me an accidental chance
To see through eyes that were not mine
Answers to questions I didn't have
But now they're there, ok... that's fine

I am so fucking blind
To think I had the day
Now I stand here posted
With nothing left to say

Who am I?
What does it matter
I am as useless as the fluid
We all drain from our bladder

I...can't...think...
what am I to do
but keep walking on my path
on my journey for the truth

Open mouth and insert foot
I am a master of that game
Do you have the same problem
Does it make you feel pain

You told me that I wasn't...
I guess that's only fair...
So now is when it happens...
I can feel that cold dark stare

HEIDI L. HART

Starting Fires

In not so many words
You told me you have no trust
Maybe it was never there
So much of nothing flushed

It doesn't matter now
I know what you really think
You can't save what was not real
So just wash it down the sink

No matter what gets tossed at us
We try to bring the joke
But tonight I feel as though
On these words I have to choke

Somewhere along the way
I got lost without a map
It's good that I am lost
Then I'm free from all the crap

It might have worked out better
Had you not handed me that book
I think I flipped one page to far
And for you that's all it took

Drag me through the mud
And I will come out clean
Feeling like I found the answer
That no one else has seen

You're a damn good teacher
I am forever learning
That some of our life lessons
Will leave you forever burning

Don't let that get you down
So much good will come from this
Even if it wasn't planned
Might be an answer to a wish

Don't look at me in pain
And think I give a care
Never my intention
Do you think that is not fair

Start some fires now
Burn up whatever you had here
I have felt my last emotion
And cried my final tear

HEIDI L. HART

Think It Over

I could kill an afternoon
Lost inside my mind
It can leave you exhausted
Make you go searching out your bed

If you've let it cross your mind
That thoughts are thoughts, and that is it
Then let me tell you this
Your about to take your biggest hit

You hold more power in one thought
Then, ten men in their hands
But if you don't follow through
It washes out just like the sands

Common sense gives us direction
Our conscience keeps us straight
Suggestion gives us option
Should I really take the bait

Looking back on where I've been
I know my thinker's played its part
Carefully, examining
Each move back from the start

I've made my share if mistakes
Because of facts I didn't know
About these people in my life
It took some time to let it show

There is no way to prepare
For the load life dumps on you
Taking one step at a time
Is the only thing that gets us through

Stand strong in your decisions
What ever they may be
You'll have a chance at better things
Coming back to you and me

If you get lost along the way
Don't let fear over come
All the progress that you've made
Take in account the things you've done

Tread lightly on one's feelings
For you would want the same
The rules need to be equal
When playing life's harsh game

HEIDI L. HART

Can't Steal Happiness

This mornings one more day
That gives insight unto me
Makes me wonder about the future
And all that it can be

Out of nowhere it appears
That thought that lives down deep
Rips and tears at my heartstrings
Creating cracks, so love shall seep

How am I suppose to feel
When I get cut right at the knees
So I have nothing left to crawl on
And its like nobody sees

Why do we have to bare
Pain, in the name of love
Love is suppose to be good
Give me the strength to rise above

Its such a tender life we live
And we're only given one
So live life to the fullest
Before, its over and done

Decisions should come easy
But yet they never do
So deep thoughts come in to play
Always be ready to think it through

It will, work itself out
Just like it always does
But, will it be the same
As it always was

I don't know this minute
Right now I really need to
So I can focus clearly
As I sit here with you

These emotions only grow
So we must know what they are
Before it goes by the wayside
Into a river like a car

Understand and then react
Make the best of what you've got
You, can not steal happiness
So don't let go of your one shot

HEIDI L. HART

Inquisitive

Inquisitive me...
Inquisitive you...
Inquisitive people...
Are in search of the truth

When thoughts run deep
And actions are small
It drives people to find
The big overall

Take my hand in this
Understand just what I feel
Let me, run through your mind
And show you what is real

Dance with inspiration
Let it take you to a place
That brings you only happiness
With a smile on your face

Let it roll right off your tongue
Just like you meant it to
Words spoken from your heart
With understanding of the truth

If God takes me tomorrow
Always believe this love we share
And if tears approach your eyes
Wipe them away without a care

Know that love is true
And that it don't die with us
That it lives in us forever
It is in this that I trust

You shall not be alone
Just reach out your heart to me
I shall hold you close inside
Until I can make you see

Do you ever wonder...
Do you think you ever will...
Or are you trapping it there...
And trying to keep it still...

Why for today
Soon see's the intensity
How finds solution
Love is complexity

HEIDI L. HART

Winter Colds

Don't you hate
Those winter colds
That make you feel
Like you are snowed

Every step you take
Feels so fricken long
You wish you could stand tall
But you aren't that strong

Walking around half asleep
Dragging on without a choice
With a godforsaken headache
Wishing you could stop the noise

Everything's an irritation
Touch, sends chills right up your spine
You want to end this misery
But your steam is quickly dying

That germ was on a mission
When it snuck up behind me
It laid the smack down, in my lungs
And now I can hardly breathe

How much more will it take
Before I get the upper hand
When I start to feeling better
Empty my shoes of all that sand

This one's got a hold on me
A bond like super glue
Misery's growing intensity
As it slowly tortures you

I'd rather have the two day flu
Non-stop chuckling and its done
This slowly attacks every part of you
Showing you everything but fun

I just wish it was over
So that I could get some rest
Sleep's the only thing that sounds good
When I am not feeling the best

My day is almost over
Soon, I'll be headed home
I will lay down to get some sleep
Right after I turn off the phone

HEIDI L. HART

My Darling Punk

My darling punk
What can I do
To show you my
True love for you

When your not here
I am not whole
I am lost completely
Mind, body, and soul

I know its been hard
The time we spend apart
But soon my love
And school will start

A new pressure will come
Putting the financials on you
But thee old one will go
Like we both want it to

I will cut most my shifts
And I'll be home at night
I think that will help...
Things to work out all right

I look into your eyes
But I can not explain
The love I have for you
Or how it drives me insane

You make me feel complete
In every single way
Showing me what love can be
Each and every single day

Self esteem, it eats us both
For neither one of us a drop
But together we move mountains
And its us no one can stop

I will never take a step
If I can't have you by my side
My life would hold no joy
Without you to share the ride

Please stay with me my love
Take my hand and be my wife
For I can not live without
The happiness you bring my life

HEIDI L. HART

Question

Question is a funny thing
The un-dying need to know
What things are and how they work
Along with where it is they go

It follows you like a shadow
Trapped inside your mind
Looking for the answers
That you may never find

It will never go away
For that is how we learn
Right questions, get right answers
Its for a better life we yearn

Thinkers suffer much pain
Always picking things apart
Never a moment without question
But in turn it makes them smart

Do you ask a lot of questions
Or do you not ask enough
If you hesitate to question
Life can become tough

You've got to find it funny
Those one's who think they know it all
They've never asked a question
In the end, you know they'll fall

A piece of you might wanna help
But it just better left alone
You don't need that kind of pain
From their attitude that's blown

Live free amongst your thoughts
For they can't be taken away
No today, not tomorrow
Not on any given day

If life becomes frustrating
Take a min, stop and think
It might help you find the answers
Or pull you back off the brink

Don't believe anything you hear
And only half of what you see
Question everything along the way
To see what your life can be

HEIDI L. HART

4 Years

I've waited such a long time
For a feeling such as this
Who knew that it was coming
That first moment when we kissed

Four years is quite a stretch
But its not long enough for me
Just the ending of a curse
On my way to destiny

You fill me up with hope
Hold me close in times of fear
Make me feel safe when I am scared
You are my everything my dear

When I was young I didn't know
What I wanted out of life
There was no way for me to know
That I would take you as my wife

Together hand in hand
We walk this road just you and me
Living out this life we built
With the love we hold you see

So let this mark one moment
Out of a million we create
Living happily together
I believe that we were fate

We are so much like each other
I can't believe we get along
But when we hit the weak spots
We're there to keep each other strong

You are my love and my companion
But at first you were my friend
Now you are all three
Right up to the very end

This is not the end of us
Just the dawn of a new day
A new adventure in the making
With obstacles along the way

I shall put to memory
Happy moments that we've had
So that I can always think of you
If I'm ever sad

HEIDI L. HART

You Can't

How can one explain
You can't you just move forth
One foot forward, then the next
Until you've made it out the door

What's on the other side
I'm not sure I wanna know
Take a breath and face your fears
You know you gotta go

How does one start all over
Erase words best left unsaid
You can't you take them with you
Up until the day your dead

You crack open that door
As the sun starts to appear
You slam it shut again
With onset overwhelming fear

How can you reclaim your life
When you can't escape your past
You can't, when you are weak
So find your strength, and do it fast

This world will not hold still
For the weak or faint of heart
Its hard at thee beginning
Every solution has its start

Don't think that they are stronger
Cuz they don't let their feelings show
They live in fear as well
They just don't want you to know

You need to find a happy thought
To hide your fear behind a smile
It will not fix the problem
But fuel your energy awhile

As you write down your life story
Please do not forget my chapter
Even if I am your lowest point
You know, you'll feel better after

You cant control your ability
To live life without regret
But you have got the power
To move forth, and just forget

HEIDI L. HART

Liz's Warning

For all you little people
Who think you have a chance
I am here to tell you
That I am more than circumstance

You sit back and make a plan
On how you might sneak in
But my girl is not a game
If she was, you would not win

You might think you really love her
Bit its all one big mistake
You will only cause her pain
Is that a chance you wanna take

What part of taken don't you get
We are together and in love
There's no trouble you can cause
We can't overcome and rise above

Play your games if you need
Maybe you will learn
That "if you play with fire
You will eventually get burned"

You've got to be a little foolish
To think that I'd just walk away
We are bonded by our love
That we take with us day to day

Try not to get me wrong
I can see why you might fall
She has been known to cause the urge
To get down on your knees and crawl

It happens just like that
I can't help but blame her hair
But she is so much more than that
And I do not intend to share

Step up to the plate my friend
If you think you got what it takes
But don't come cry to me
When it's your heart that she breaks

I will just step back now
I do not wish to disturb
The entertaining event of
You getting kicked to the curb

HEIDI L. HART

Giddy

One look was all it took
Melted me, is what you've done
With your hot ass banging body
You make me crave a little fun

When I'm sitting all alone
I get these random thoughts of you
I get feeling so damn giddy
About the things I wanna do

I wanna put my hands all over you
In an oh, so gentle way
That will give you an inner tingle
Lasting long throughout the day

I sit inside anticipating
The next time I'll see you
Daytime seems so long
And its hard to make it through

You have become my happy thought
No matter what tries to get me down
You pick me up, and stand me tall
And wipe away that frown

I have this over whelming warmth
From my head down to my toes
Holding this great power over me
That nobody else knows

One wish come true for me
When you wrap your arms around
Pull me in, to hold me close
No better feeling has been found

I can't even clear my mind of you
When I have things I need to do
It makes me wonder at times
If you have that problem too

It sets heavy like a ton of bricks
That thought that we were meant to be
As time goes on that thought gets stronger
Opening my eyes up to what I see

Lets hold on to this feeling
It feels to good to let it go
I open up these feelings to you
Cuz I thought, you might wanna know

HEIDI L. HART

Frustrations Freedom

Don't let the sun go down
On this kind of frustration
Anger in this form
Holds no permanent position

If I die tomorrow
Would you still be feeling hate
Or be to late to accept my apology
I guess that's just my fate

I wish that misunderstandings
Would never come my way
But they happen, that's just life
Don't let them ruin your day

I wish I could bring to words
A solution to ease your mind
But it just don't come out right
I shall look one more time

A peace keeper in the wings
That is what I seem to be
So what is it here
I'm failing to see

My job in life is still unknown
So possible location is unclear
Take my hand and be my friend
Together, we will make it dear

There's nothing we can't do
As long as we give it a try
Put forth our strongest effort
Up until the day we die

I know it can be hard
To keep the faith when you are down
But good times always come
Eliminating your frown

We can not control the past
Just adjust our point of view
Sometimes it is the only way
For us to make it through

Open up your arms
And let the freedom rein
It might not fix it all
But it will ease the pain

HEIDI L. HART

Left Field

I think I need a minute
Maybe I'm wrong it might be 2
Confusions running thick
And I'm not sure what to do

Look one way, there stands trouble
Look another and there's more
I try reaching out for help
At every turn one more locked door

Stand in my slippers for a second
Is fuzzy what you feel
My vision is so blurry
I can't tell if this is real

Driving blind into a snowstorm
Not quite sure what's up ahead
My fear grows bigger every minute
That before its over I'll be dead

Just about the time
I think I got it back on track
I have whittled down my problems
Just to find another stack

Please God, send me the answer
Or point me to what is right
Trapped out on this broken bridge
I have been out here all night

I feel fatigue, its coming on
Not of body, but of soul
Trying to locate the truth
Is like climbing a greased pole

I know good things take time
And sometimes a little space
But I feel I'm getting nowhere
Moving at this slowed down pace

Take my hand and pull me up
I can not do this on my own
Breaking a trail into this life
Is something I have to be shown

It took me an extra minute
But I thank you for your hand
I could not do it alone
You've taught me how to make a stand

HEIDI L. HART

I'll Never Know

In search of words
I can not find
In search of truth's...
Way out of this bind

How did I get here
Where'd it all go
What did I do
Someone must know

This must be a dream
There's no way this is real
Can you even confir
With this confusion I feel

I am in very great fear
But, I do not know why
It's like a scary movie
You just know your gonna die

You take a step forward
And the shots start to fire
No way to side step
When walking a wire

I'm not asking for much
Or maybe I am
But how will I know
If I don't make a stand

A small bit of perspective
That you must possess
I might be in lack of
An amount of caress

Think long and act quick
These are the rules of the game
You're the one in control
So no room to place blame

Figure out what is real
And what's there for show
If I do not proceed
Then I'll never know

Why I woke up this morning
On my living room floor
Laying half in...
And out of, my front door

HEIDI L. HART

Stop To Think

Do you ever stop to think
I've done it once or twice
It got me in some trouble
And not treated very nice

Sometimes a second thought
Will help you work your problems through
Sometimes it's the bullet
That puts and end to you

Not knowing what is right
Are weak words we do not say
They hold no credibility
When mapping out your way

Slap down that do not cross sign
Put up resistance I can't fight
I will figure out a master plan
To get to what I know is right

Lead on, if you need to
But I've got this in hand
Traveling on now
To the plentiful land

To where all is green
With a beauty so true
But it still means nothing
If I'm here without you

Perfection is not real
It is happiness I crave
So it will be to love
That I shall remain a slave

I am in hot pursuit
To just stop, and turn around
Be it all and everything at once
Is a miracle seldom found...

Leaving me tore down
I shall not let it win
Or drag me through the swamps
That lead only to sin

So once more, I'll stop to think
Look back on a thing or two
Until I'm locked on solidly
And have cut a path on through

No Point

No point in searching
For what's left of me
I loose every battle
That I'm sent to beat

Used up and worthless
Is what I've become
I guess that's how I know
My work has to be done

You can't rely on me
So don't even try
The world might be better
If I were to die

An old piece of crap
Needing kicked to the curb
Ever so gently now
So your not to disturb

Those good folks who know
How to make every turn
But do not have the time
To try and help me learn

It is ok though
It is not their job
To help me regain
What I was once robbed

Spit on me
Throw your stones
Curse my name
And break my bones

It's all a rerun
That goes on in my head
When I lay down to sleep
Alone in my bed

I felt a cold chill
Just shoot up my spine
Not sure why it came on
At least not this time

So often I look
For an answer... no luck
Down further I sink
Permanently stuck

HEIDI L. HART

Jo-Jo

Stop once, and look back
On amazing times we've had
If I had to face loosing them
It would make me forever sad

You are my strength
In times of need
It is on you
My love shall feed

When I need to sit and cry
Just so I can get it out
Your there to keep me calm
So that I loose my urge to shout

I could not make one step forward
If I knew you were not there
If I had to wake up alone
I'd just loose my will to care

You are what brightens up my day
Without a doubt why I have hope
When we face our toughest battles
You are why I fight to cope

You are my blanket when I'm cold
My teddy bear when I need to sleep
Off and dreaming peacefully
Without a single peep

No way for me to pay you back
For everything you've given me
You are my one blessing
Even if you can not see

On the brink of something good
My life is perfect with you here
My goal now, is forever
Can you handle that my dear

Your smiles are like calories
As I pack on the pounds of love
With no urge to lose the weight
But just a hope that it goes up

You are my everything
That makes me feel right
Throughout the long days
And night after night

Time Coming

Back at work again
Wishing I was there with you
My minds in hyper overdrive
Of these things I wanna do

It's killing me to be awake
When your so far away
Time slows down when you are waiting
For the sun to start your day

So trapped inside my thoughts
Of making, such sweet love to you
You lost in peaceful dreaming
I know that you want it too

There are so very many things
That I don't think we'll get the time
I'm gonna make them fit somehow
At least give it my best try

Before I left the house tonight
I saw that look upon your face
The one that shows how bad
You need me close for warm embrace

I could not start before I left
I don't wanna stop half through
I need the time to take it slow
Just like I know you'd want me too

Kiss-kiss... good night..., I love you dear
I will see you in the morn
Cause tonight when you get home
The ropes are off... I'm in rare form

We'll start off slow and tease a bit
As I climb up on top
There will be words that you scream
But not one of them is STOP!

I wanna start your day off right
With these words to make you smile
To fill your day with happy thoughts
That will stick around awhile

It wont be long and you'll be home
Our time is coming hun
Work wont last long then you'll be here
And we can have a little fun

HEIDI L. HART

100% Pure

Like pen and paper
Is how you phrased it to me
I agree with you love
The rest just can't see

This thing that we have
Between me and you
Is sweeter than sugar
Time's showed it true

When I become sick
And do not feel good
You nurse me back to health
To make me feel like I should

We have our problems
Just like everyone else
But their always worked out
Together we take the steps

I use to think fate
Just could not be real
You've ended that thought
With the way you make me feel

You've given me love
No one else could provide
Come what may, you've been there
To stand strong at my side

My best moments come
When I pass out in your arms
Falling asleep knowing
That I'm safe from all harms

When I wake in the morning
Looking deep into your eyes
I feel I'm closer to heaven
Then the clouds in the skies

One more thing I ask
If that's ok with you
Given back in equal value
That is my promise too

It is that promise of forever
Not with the court, but with your heart
Take my hand and accept my love
And promise that we'll never part

HEIDI L. HART

Carry On

It all starts here
But why you ask
It's the only way
To complete your task

You can not run
From what must be
Find the truth
So you can see

Sometimes you must lose
In order to gain
You were never promised
That it wouldn't cause pain

But stay strong ...
And stay true ...
Don't do it for others
It must be for you

In the end you'll be glad
That you stayed on the path
For, the punishment for wandering
Brings on a heavy wrath

With a moments notice
Or no notice at all
It can be all gone
And there starts your fall

Right now we're here
So many choices at hand
Careful thought makes it clear
Behind which ones you should stand

Have faith in yourself
That you know right away
It shall come back to you
At the end of the day

These moments don't last
So enjoy what you can
Don't waste all your time
Trying to draw out a plan

Let your heart lead you
Destination unknown
To the place you eventually
Come to call home

HEIDI L. HART

Mr. Wiggles

The day my buddy
Tried to burn a worm
He started to wiggle
He started to squirm

Inch by inch
Away from the flame
There's nobody here
But Mandy to blame

Put him on the run
Just out of spite
I think she was trying
To shorten his life

He kept on crawling
Till he was out of view
Watch out little friend
She's following you

A moment of rest
Is all your gonna find
For insects and crawlers
Her heart is not kind

Her smoke break is over
So hear comes your head start
But she's gonna dump trash soon
So watch out for her cart

I know this ain't fair
To be drawn out by the rain
And be in sight of this woman
Who thinks your death is a game

If you can hold out
For a couple more hours
The sun will be out
You can hide back in the flowers

I guess this is my fault
For pointing you out to her
How was I to know
That she'd set you to burn

All has worked out
You've survived the night
My only suggestion to you
Is to stay out of sight

HEIDI L. HART

Pinch

How do we end up here
Time after time
Searching out pennies
To make one more dime

It won't get you to far
But its all that you got
To try and pull you
From this uncomfortable spot

I open the fridge
And what's left to see
One last cup of milk
Two eggs and some tea

One last meal my dear boy
Mommies doing her best
But our financial position
Has put me to the test

With each passing day
We'll share feelings of love
And it will be the one thing
That helps us rise above

Someday it'll be better
I just can't tell you when
I pray you stick by me
Between now and then

These times don't come often
When they do it is bad
With no positive outlook
It'll make you feel sad

One day at a time
And with each step we take
We will start to improve
On the decisions we make

We cut this one close
But we'll make it my dear
Moving forth hand in hand
Facing this with no fear

Life will always throw stones
But strength is a must
Just have faith in our love
It's the one thing you can trust

HEIDI L. HART

Stage Fright

I can feel it coming on
A case of stage fright is at hand
My knees are getting weak
And I don't know if I can stand

I look out across the room
Two hundred people is what I see
I could picture them naked
But their still staring at me

I was sure that I could do this
Before I got up on stage
But now that I am here
I feel my fear begin to rage

I feel a silence sweeping over me
And I had so much to say
This is just not how I pictured it
When I started out my day

I came here to share some stories
Laugh and joke a little bit
But now I feel so faint
I think all I can do is sit

I don't know why this took me over
I'm not usually like this
Sharing poetry with new friends
Is what gives me inner bliss

How long have I been standing here
With these tears rolling down my face
For this, I've waited such a long time
Now I feel so outta place

Someone stop the world and let me off
I can not take this fast pace spin
Things were working out just fine
Till I got caught by this whirl wind

Time to take a minute
Stop it all, and just reflect
All the things that brought me here
Are in these books that I collect

Can someone here please help me
Stop this ringing in my ear
"Heidi" "honey, wake up"
It was only a nightmare

HEIDI L. HART

Turn It Up

Happy songs help us
When we are depressed
Help us walk the line
When we are upset

If you hear a little jingle
Perk your ears it might be good
Speed things up that have slowed down
Get things moving like they should

Break out in dance
No one's around
Break out in song
YEAH!! That's the sound

When the music gets a rollin
Bob your head to that rich beat
It will rock all through your body
As it drives into your feet

You can't help but sing along
With a smile ear to ear
A song with so much power
You have simply got to hear

Come on in the more the merry
I feel a party start to brew
So crank up the music
There's no better thing to do

Don't fight the feeling coming on
It'll leave you begging for more
As you shimmy through the crowd
On your way to thee dance floor

First you grab a partner
Then when you start to jive
Look around the room
As this whole place becomes alive

Letting good times roll
You are here amongst good friends
We are gonna keep it rockin
Up until this party ends

I'm so glad we've had this time to share
Some happiness through song
My only hope at this point
Is that it lingers all night long

HEIDI L. HART

Dragging

Tonight is just one of those
Nights I can't bare
I want to reach up
And pull out my hair

This one wants pain pills
And can't have one now
That one wants dressed
And claims he don't know how

Keep slapping that call light
I know your confused
I'm loosing my patience
Because I'm not amused

It takes a little inner strength
To get through days like these
I would do most anything
Even get down on my knees

Rounds are coming up again
And I just wanna run
I know I'll be back in there
And it wont be any fun

There is, no cure for a long night
You just take them step by step
Hope some where along the way
You can gain a little pep

I sit here looking through the cracks
Where my eyes use to be
I wish I wasn't so damn tired
It really makes it hard on me

From somewhere in the distance
Comes this beeping in my ear
I look up to see a red light
It's a call light that I hear

One foot and then another
I start out down that long hall
Trying to maintain some balance
So that I don't trip and fall

Every step feels like a million
Every second ticks so slow
Like your night's come to a stop
And all you want is just to go

HEIDI L. HART

One Stipulation

So many times
I have been told
I am in the wrong field
My work needs to be sold

I would not mind sharing
Confidence, my weak spot
I don't think I could compete
With so many good ones at the top

Maybe sometime in the future
I could publish one or two
Even if I reached that goal
Would it be enough for you

I have such a hard time
Believing that you wanna hear
The echo's of my life
Ringing down into your ear

No one thinks their someone
Until someone thinks they are
Then one day you wake up
And you have become a star

Curiosity of that process
Is what makes us all unique
Go in search of just one person
That'll take the time to just critique

One ear that will listen
One eye that ain't gone blind
One mind that will stay open
Can be really hard to find

Fear of what could happen
If I let my secrets go
The pain one could inflict on me
If I let those feelings show

Locked up for so many years
Word for word inside a book
Afraid to let it out
For it's my life, that would be shook

So step by step I'll take the chance
Let them out into the world
The only thing I ask
Is you not hurt this little girl

HEIDI L. HART

Frozen

Sitting here right now
I can only think of you
The plan we've made for our future
And all the things we wanna do

I've never been so happy
As I've been these last five years
If I'm ever to cry again
Then they're to be only happy tears

Time apart drives me insane
You're why I get out of bed
And even when I can not see you
You are what fills my head

When I think of where I've been
And all the years I've lost
Spending time with hateful people
Paying out emotional cost

I know now where I belong
Here with you right by my side
Not one thing could turn me back
Not even the strongest ocean tide

Your arms wrapped around me
Is like a sunrise of the heart
I'll pray seven times a day
If it means we'll never have to part

I'd miss everything we have
The things that one can not possess
Your love, your touch, your pretty face
Your soft simple caress

When your not here I spend my minutes
Thinking of things we're gonna do
Just anything that gets me
Curled up right next to you

I'm frozen from a love spell
That you have put on me
Loving every moment
Never past it will I be

Right here, right now together
Will you place your hand in mine
I'll give you my promise
Of my love for all of time

HEIDI L. HART

Truth Hurts

You lying mother fucker
You think I can't see past your lies
You should count yourself lucky
I gave you, this many tries

I know that when I go to work
Your with another bitch
Trying to rub up on her softly
Just to cure your manly itch

You don't want me to leave
But yet you do it every night
Not even caring for a moment
That it will cause another fight

I used to think I loved you
Now the sight of you, just makes me sick
I think you better keep your distance
Or I might just cut off your dick

You think that you're a player
And I am just part of the game
When really you're a piece of shit
That deserves all of the blame

With everyday that passes
I hate you more and more
Now here's the reality son
I'm walking out the door

I am never looking back
For there is nothing there to see
You gave away so much of you
That there was nothing left for me

Bitches, ho's and tramps alike
They're gonna make see
But maybe it wont happen
Till the give you HIV

Say what you feel you need to
You can't make me turn around
As shitty as you make me feel
A better life is easy found

C'est la vie you fuckin prick
I don't care what becomes of you
I'm on my way to happiness
Aren't you glad you know the truth

HEIDI L. HART

The Start

After all this time together
There's one thing I've learned from you
That's to select my words carefully
For the fear of what you'll do

I think most of it's my fault
Always picking things apart
I just don't wanna cause you pain
With feeble matters of the heart

What good can come from verbal fight
It just leaves us both not talking
You do so much better now
At least you don't just take off walking

You mean so much to me my love
So my arguing days are through
Life don't give us to much time
I want mine making memories with you

Good one's that will make me smile
Every time you cross my mind
You gave me every thing I want
What more is there to find

Pebbles in the road my sweet
Just need to kick them out of the way
They mean nothing to our future
Their only moments in our day

I look past your jealousy
Cause I have it real bad too
But if I let it take me over
It will only cost me you

You and I are twins of time
Anger eats us both alive
So these steps we make together
Are for the better life we strive

This is to be the challenge
For no good thing, comes free
We must apply good effort
Together you and me

We proclaim our love day in day out
So lets give it all our heart
Don't give up on ,me baby
This only just the start

HEIDI L. HART

Secret Agent

You are a super secret agent
Every day comes one more truth
Your title might be LPN
But we all call you Ruth

A figure of astonishment
Intelligence with no end
We could search this world forever
And never find a better friend

I've never met a person
Who could pull me from my doubt
You are like fresh rain to a field
That's been suffering a drought

So many times I've come to work
Unable to fight my tears
And without a single word
You've taught me how to face my fears

There are just so many sides to you
That I didn't know about
But one step at a time
We are slowly being taught

A nurse with such experience
I know you've seen your share of trauma
But starting out I didn't know
You were a motorcycle mama

My past has slowly taught me
I should trust within a limit
But there isn't one damn thing
I wouldn't tell you in a minute

One of the few that has believed in me
I am so glad that we met
If all my friends were just like you
Then my life would be set

A buddy in the length of things
Always there to help me through
I got to break in my new chainsaw
And that thanks goes out to you

I shall always have a smile
For my secret agent friend
Locked away for times safe keeping
So I'll still have it in the end

HEIDI L. HART

Feeling Blah

I really love my job
But tonight I don't feel good
I hope that it stays calm
And things go as they should

I am usually full of energy
But right now I'm dragging tail
If only I could put some wind
Up underneath my sail

I just have no ambition
For the things I need to do
I wanna clock out and come home
So I can curl up next to you

It's hard to start your day
When you are feeling sick
You keep digging in that bag
To try and pull out one last trick

Now starts the count down
Only five hours left to go
Will my feet carry me that long
It is this I do not know

I take it with a bag of salt
Because a grain was not enough
When you get wore down this far
You got to stand, and just be tough

We all have bad days
That will pop up now and then
But we must find our will
1 foot in front of the other again

I know that it wont last forever
This day will come to an end
I just hope it does it soon
Because my body's already spent

We do what we have to do
There is no other way
To take care of our family
If you don't drag on through this day

Here we go a second wind
Hold on tight and take a breath
Even though you wanna stop
And all over feel like death

HEIDI L. HART

It's All You

A moment of desperation
One that leaves us with no choice
But to stand and give the truth
With a firm yet gentle voice

We all see different sides
They'll all tell a different tale
There is only one here strong enough
To stop the evil before we fail

Why be lost amongst the cotton
We've beaten down a trail for you
Don't put to much thought into it
Just set forth and tell the truth

25 people trapped inside
With one person at fault
When they step forward on their own
There's one good lesson being taught

Situation is irrelevant
It's about how we respond
Doing what is right
It is of reason I am fond

There aren't that many people
Who still believe in good within
They think the world is full of
Wrong doers and of sin

There are still a few of us
That believe in what is right
A few that can sleep peacefully
When they lay down their head at night

It don't take a congregation
Groups are for those who cant see
I tend to think better alone
Less corruption, when it's just me

Live your life just how you will
But remember my dear friend
Regret and consequence
Seem to run hand in hand

That is not an ultimatum
Just a thought to keep in mind
When your in search of something
That you cant seem to find

HEIDI L. HART

Rocking Chairs On Fire

Way back when we got started
I took you , to have to hold
But all your idiosyncrasies
Are getting a little old

I use to love you in so many ways
Now your ways drive me insane
To a point I wanna reach out
And give you a little pain

You cause me such frustration
The way you think you rule the roost
Just wait until I give you
Foot to ass, a giant boost

We should be growing old together
But I got the house, you got the shop
It's probably good we're separated
Or I'd have brought us to a stop

I'm sure we'll make it through
Given time and given space
I won't have reason for anger
As long, as you stay out of my face

Over time my love has weakened
To the point, I believe no more
My peaceful moments come
When I see you, walk out the door

I use to think that it was you and I
But now your cycles run through your life
I guess your papa never taught you
Just how you should treat your wife

With everyday comes one more struggle
Just to make it through the day
Without speaking words that hurt
That I so often want to say

Young lovers always picture
Rocking chairs, set side by side
Now I fall asleep questioning
Why for so long I have tried

So for you these words of truth
I'm just trying to keep it real
Without to many words of hatred
It's just how you make me feel

HEIDI L. HART

Love's Pain

Lately I cant get you
Off of my mind for a minute
Like the way the world wont stop
It just keeps right on ah spinnin

I worry about you constantly
And how things will work out
I know your at peak frustration
To a point you wanna shout

Think of me as your forever
I am never far behind you
And I am always gonna be there
To do my best to help you through

You've got so many friends in this
That are beside you in this choice
We're going to pull you clear
Of this fires physical voice

It will take some time to heal
For your pain to go away
Just know that I'll still be here
When you come upon that day

I am living breathing prove
You're a maker of good things
You will make plenty more
Just watch what the future brings

We all suffer pain in life
That doesn't seem to fair
It's the remnants of lost love
Caused by the breaking of a pair

We can not for-see the future
To stop the pain before the start
So when things take a wrong turn
We have to sacrifice and part

Live and learn is what they call it
Emotions we are forced to feel
Tear us down then stand us up
And then teach us how to deal

How ever it works out
We must keep looking onward dear
Try to stay strong and focused
Do not be overcome by fear

HEIDI L. HART

Random Thoughts

I wanna stop a minute
Have a random thought or two
Bring it out into the air
And discuss it all with you

What is a random thought you ask
Unanswered questions on the brain
The one's that make you ask twice
And leave you, feeling insane

Like if you take a shower
Why's the towel considered dirty
If you would hang it up
Then you might not go through thirty

I cant help but ask these questions
They are there and so am I
It is to darn irresistible
To ask the question why

It's that burning itch inside of me
That has really gotta know
Those useless bits of information
The general public just don't show

How is it, that we're here
With these questions in our head
Don't they bother you at all
When you try to go to bed

Some don't give a squat
Let alone a second thought
I guess it doesn't matter
If their not wanting to be taught

If we all took a minute
To share idea's on senseless things
We could clear out some confusion
And take flight with lighter wings

So next time someone asks you
How you put on your pants
Give them an honest answer
Instead, of a hateful glance

Together we take baby steps
Into the way beyond and more
Looking for a little insight
To what's behind the secret door

HEIDI L. HART

Mental Slime

I can't stop the inner ticking
That's going on inside of me
My thoughts are jumping like electrons
Hoping I will set them free

Just going on about my day
It's like multiple voices in my head
And the only rest I get
Is when I lay down to bed

Most of the time, I have to stop
And just pick up my pen
Slow them down and sort them out
Write them down then start again

Try not to get me wrong
I really love to write
But with so many thoughts at once
It's like the voices like to fight

These thoughts start when I get busy
Its like they know I don't have time
So they slip right through my fingers
Like some form of mental slime

Some of them are really good
But I'll never get them back
If I did then I'd have books
Clear to the ceiling in a stack

I like it better this way
Each poem I write means more to me
I think they'd lose some value
If I wrote, in mass quantity

So to prevent the loss of good ones
I'll write down a simple phrase
To help it to come back to me
Sometime in my future days

For all the one's I lost
I'm not sure were meant to be
I am still here waiting
If you want... come back to me

I will never be so busy
That I can't take the time
To capture one more moment
And write it down in form of rhyme

HEIDI L. HART

Free To Re-gain

The moment that I think
I've cried my last tear drop
I take another look to see
That I never really stopped

We grow and we learn
Most every day
But strength is a choice
What more can I say

What you do , where you go
Your decision at hand
The choice builds your will
So behind it you'll stand

Weak when alone
I stand strong for you
So you can leave knowing
My feelings are true

I'll miss you with everything
I hold inside of me
For when you return
Once again I shall see

Distance is good
At this moment in life
To free you from stress
Mental torture and strife

Soon you'll release
And become who you need
No longer be held back
Re-learn to take lead

Independence and strength
Have always been your strong suit
So this is just a small set back
As you get back on route

Things will get better
One step at a time
And you will gain balance
To walk this thin line

At the end you'll be happy
You have stepped out into...
The world and you've brought
Your children back to you

HEIDI L. HART

The Code

A –   B –   C –   D –   E –   F –

G –   H –   I –   J –   K –   L –

M –   N –   O –   P –   Q –   R –

S –   T –   U –   V –   W –

X –   Y –   Z –